The Label Reader's
POCKET DICTIONARY
of FOOD ADDITIVES

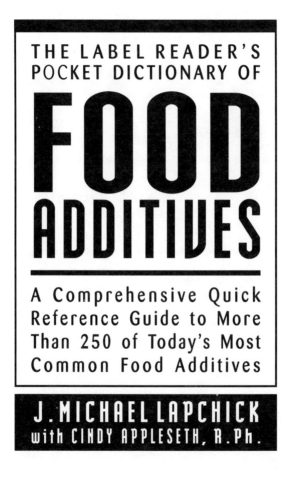

THE LABEL READER'S POCKET DICTIONARY OF

FOOD ADDITIVES

A Comprehensive Quick Reference Guide to More Than 250 of Today's Most Common Food Additives

J. MICHAEL LAPCHICK
with CINDY APPLESETH, R.Ph.

The Label Reader's Pocket Dictionary of Food Additives
Copyright © 1993 by J. Michael Lapchick

Library of Congress Cataloging-in-Publication Data
Lapchick, J. Michael
      The label reader's pocket dictionary
         of food additives / J. Michael Lapchick
         with Cindy Appleseth.
         p.   cm.
ISBN 1-56561-027-X: $4.95
  **1. Food additives—Dictionaries.   I. Appleseth, Cindy.
II. Title**
TX553.A3L35 1993
664'.06'03—dc20   93-12765
                       CIP

Edited by Jeff Braun
Design by MacLean & Tuminelly
Production Coordination by Claire Lewis
Printed in the United States of America.

10 9 8 7 6 5 4 3 2 1

Published by:
CHRONIMED Publishing
P.O. Box 47945
Minneapolis, MN 55447-9727

The Label Reader's
POCKET DICTIONARY
of FOOD ADDITIVES

This book is not meant as a definitive guide to food additives. Rather, it is intended to provide a summary of available information on the subject. You should consult a health professional if you are concerned about the food you eat.

Contents

This book is dedicated
to my mom and dad . . .
they know why.

Special thanks to James Barnard for all his research
assistance and patience, aisle after aisle, and to Laura
Barton for her love and support.

J. M. Lapchick

Introduction

I live on the outskirts of a suburb set in a valley. When my family moved here over 20 years ago, one of the east coast's first shopping malls was being built in a beautiful but empty rock quarry. A few miles away from us was farmland.

On hot Sundays after church we'd stop at the arboretum where the township kept up the old Black Hawk Spring—a sort of roadside novelty. We couldn't wait to taste that cool, fresh spring water pumping from the earth.

You'd never know it, but seven miles away in the next town over is one of the country's larger oil refineries. We don't see it, hear it, or smell it. It's not even a part of our life. Or, at least, we thought it wasn't.

But when the drinking water in that town became unsafe from pollution and general abuse, some of the people there found our Black Hawk Spring. It quickly became a source of fresh water for hundreds of families. For years, people lined up every day carrying jugs in every shape and size. The township even widened the parking lot and opened more spouts.

Now I can't stop for a simple drink anymore—not because of the crowds, but because the Black Hawk Spring was shut down this past fall. Why? They say the groundwater is contaminated.

In an age where pollution and chemicals are so irrevocably woven into our lives, it's critical to educate ourselves. We need to make healthy choices. Otherwise, we're at the mercy of our often unfriendly surroundings.

We know some chemicals in our food and air are hazardous; some have been proven to cause cancer. It's practically impossible to *completely* escape them. However, we can make adjustments to improve our health today and safeguard us from possible harm tomorrow.

EXPECTATIONS

A certain trust is implied every time we pick a product off the shelf and put it in our grocery carts. We trust the label reads true. We also trust the ingredients are safe, sanitary, and desirable. But as we scan the list of ingredients and they become less and less familiar, we are asked to trust a little more. What about those ingredients we can't even pronounce? Should we assume the products must be safe if they made it to the supermarket? Where do we turn if we want a product with more familiar ingredients?

Most of us know the dangers of fat, cholesterol, and sodium. Now you can add food additives to your list of concerns. But with a little knowledge, or at least a resource such as this book, you can start shopping with more confidence. Once you evaluate and adjust your consumption of additives, you might find yourself with a little more energy and clarity you didn't even realize were missing.

I stopped eating most additives about five years ago. It wasn't immediate, but after four months I noticed my short-term memory had improved. I no longer walked into rooms without knowing why. Before, I had always been accused of being absent-minded; losing my keys and wallet, forgetting names and things people said. When I began to monitor and change my eating habits, most of this cloud seemed to lift. It was subtle, but definite.

A year ago I was on a rather lengthy airplane trip. I had forgotten (well, maybe I am a bit absent-minded) to call ahead for a vegetarian meal, which, although I'm not a vegetarian, is about the best one can do in hope of a healthy meal during a flight. Lunch was a ham and cheese sandwich, a turkey sandwich, or nothing at all. I hadn't eaten all morning, and I figured one ham and cheese wouldn't kill me.

I have to admit, it tasted pretty good. But it was hardly worth the three hours of memorable gas and diarrhea that followed. Nobody else got sick. I know now it was the chemicals in the processed lunch meat. Although I'm sure I could train my body to eat that way again, this and other similar instances prove chemicals do not belong in my body.

J. M. Lapchick

WIDESPREAD USE

Food additives have been around for hundreds of years. Originally, their use was limited to preserving meats and other perishables. However, in the 1900s, particularly after World War II, food manufacturers began to look for ways to market their fresh products nationwide. Products not only had to be fresh, but look and feel fresh, too.

The manufacturers turned to chemical companies. Additives allowed food companies to grow by expanding distribution, taking business from local butchers and farmers. The public became so conditioned by cosmetically-enhanced, highly-advertised products that eating anything else was almost unheard of.

But things seem to be changing. As the country's health awareness continues to grow, the market for all-natural products is growing. More and more alternative products are finding their way to the shelves, and people are buying them.

And yes, they're finding those products in general supermarkets. It just takes some careful shopping.

Health food stores also are an excellent source of all-natural products.

This book was researched and written with the shopper in mind. All the additives listed are in popular products sold in most supermarkets. Thousands of pages of information have been carefully abridged in a concise format making this book the perfect shopping companion.

UNFAMILIAR NAMES

Too often, food additive names are intimidating or misleading. For instance, a product that contains sodium chloride, inositol, and 7-dehydrocholesterol might concern you, until you learn they are nothing more than common table salt and vitamins B and D_3.

On the other hand, a product containing brominated vegetable oil (BVO) might seem perfectly harmless. However, BVO has been proven to cause organ degeneration and central nervous system problems. *The Label Reader's Pocket Dictionary of Food Additives* will help you determine what foods are acceptable to you.

Five basic questions are answered for each additive whenever possible:

1. **Are its origins natural,
    or is it synthetically produced?**

    Additives can be manufactured by nature, with little or no processing, or by scientists, made entirely from chemical compounds, or any combination of both. A natural origin in no way ensures an additive's safety, nor does a synthetic compound automatically pose a threat.

2. **What is its purpose?**

    Some additives serve different purposes in different foods. They are referred to as multi-purpose by the Food and Drug Administration (FDA). You'll find only the most common uses listed in this book. Definitions of uses are included in the glossary. Often a food additive will also be put in cosmetics or have an industrial use. You won't find that purpose here because there's no need to confuse or frighten you unnecessarily. For more information about other uses of food additives, refer to the bibliography.

3. In what foods is it commonly found?

Obviously not all foods containing a particular additive can be listed. However, the information provided will give you a sense of the types of foods in which you might expect to find it.

4. Does it pose a health hazard?

Many problems occur when trying to determine an additive's safety because there are so many variables. For instance, there's the possible hazard of mixing additives. Over 8,000 additives are used in food. And it's nearly impossible to test all the combinations to see if they are toxic.

Another problem is that toxicity information is available for only about half of all food additives. Furthermore, research is done to determine an additive's carcinogenicity (tendency to cause cancer), but few tests explore the effects on the brain and nervous system.

When an additive has many pages of clinical findings available, this book summarizes only the most conclusive evidence. Often toxicity information is vague and incomplete. For example, a preservative may be proven safe when injected under the skin of dogs, monkeys, and frogs, but may cause cancerous tumors in rats. In this instance, the entry would state "safety is questionable." You may want to refer to the bibliography for more information.

Many of the sources used in this book are available from your local book store (with the exception of FDA publications and more technical works which can be found at most university libraries).

At the left of each entry is one of three symbols to give you a quick overview. These symbols are only a graphic representation of the

information at hand and not a definitive rating.
They are:

= Not known to be toxic

= Safety is questionable
and/or poorly tested

= Probable health hazard

As convenient as the dictionary listings are, the
"safety ratings at a glance" section (page 93)
offers an even quicker overview of additive safety.
Additives are grouped together by name only,
according to the three categories: safe, questionable, or a probable health hazard.

5. **What is its FDA status?**

You'll find the acronym GRAS (Generally Recog-
nized As Safe) at the end of some entries. The
GRAS (pronounced "grass") rating was first given
to a group of additives in 1958. These substances
had been widely used with no signs of harmful
effects. They were assumed to be safe and therefore exempt from any further testing.

Unfortunately, many items on the original list were poorly tested or not tested at all. In the 1970s, the FDA started to reevaluate GRAS substances. Several additives such as cyclamates (artificial sweeteners) lost their GRAS status. FDA approval has come a long way since the 1950s.

Today, a new additive first must pass tests required by the FDA. The tests are performed by the chemical manufacturer and evaluated by the FDA. If the results are accepted, the compound is granted a "regulated" status and can be used in food. If the manufacturer wants to pursue a GRAS rating, which may make it more enticing to food companies, it must publish the test results in certain journals and publications. Still, a GRAS status does not necessarily mean an additive is completely risk-free.

Food Additives (A to Z)

ACACIA GUM (gum arabic)   Obtained from tree native to parts of Africa. Used as a thickener and also as an emulsifier to prevent separation. Found in candy, soft drinks, and chewing gum. Some allergic reactions have been reported. Vegetable gums are poorly tested but present no apparent danger. GRAS

ACESULFAME POTASSIUM (acesulfame-K, Sunette®)   A synthetic sugar substitute 200 times sweeter than table sugar. Comparable to aspartame (NutraSweet®) in sweetness. It has no nutritional value, so it is not metabolized in the system and passes through the body unchanged. Found in sugar free gum and candy. It has been approved for use in many countries. FDA animal testing found negative toxicity results; however, some consumer groups question its safety.

ACESULFAME-K   See acesulfame potassium

ACETIC ACID (vinegar acid)   Found naturally in dairy products, fruit, and coffee. Acetic acid is the main ingredient of vinegar. Used in food as an acidulant to aid in processing, a flavor enhancer, and a curing agent to stabilize color or preserve. One of the top 50 chemicals produced in the United States. Concentrated, it is a skin and tissue irritant. Known to cause cancer in rats when injected in high doses. GRAS

ADENOSINE 5   Organic powder made from derivatives of muscle tissue or yeast. Produces energy and promotes muscular activity. Commonly found in baby formula. Not known to be toxic.

ADIPIC ACID (hexanedioic acid)   A synthetic multi-use additive similar to a compound found naturally in beets. One of the top 50 chemicals produced in the United States. Used primarily as a flavor enhancer and an acidulant to aid in processing. It is commonly found in gelatin pudding desserts and candy. Not known to be toxic. GRAS

ALGAE   See alginates

ALGINATES (algin, algin derivative, algin gum, alginic acid, ammonium alginate, calcium alginate, potassium alginate, sodium alginate, propylene glycol alginate, algae)   Obtained from seaweed. Alginates act as stabilizers, texturizers, and thickeners. They also help maintain desirable textures in dairy products. Sodium alginate's safety is questionable for pregnant women. GRAS

ALUMINUM COMPOUNDS (aluminum ammonium sulfate, aluminum chloride, aluminum hydroxide, aluminum oleate, aluminum palmitate, aluminum potassium sulfate, aluminum sulfate)   Compounds of aluminum, which is found abundantly in the earth's crust. Used as a firming agent to retain crispness, acidity controller, and clarifier to make products clear. There is evidence that aluminum may cause adverse behavioral changes, lowered strength, and sluggishness. The effects may be enhanced when combined with citrates. Also, elevated levels of aluminum were found in the brains of Alzheimer's victims, though any correlation has not yet been proven. Some studies suggest aluminum contamination may be caused in infants through baby formula. GRAS

AMINO ACIDS   The building blocks for protein. Eight of the twenty-two known amino acids are essential for the maintenance of good health and are not manufactured by the body sufficiently. Therefore, they are added to food as a dietary supplement. They are: tryptophan, phenylalanine, lysine, threonine, methionine, leucine, isoleucine, and valine. They are restricted to foods that contain protein. Not known to be toxic, except for sufferers of PKU who must avoid phenylalanine.

AMMONIUM ALGINATE   See alginates

AMMONIUM CASEINATE   See caseinates

AMMONIUM PHOSPHATE   See phosphates

AMMONIUM SALT COMPOUNDS (ammonium bicarbonate, ammonium carbonate, ammonium chloride, ammonium hydroxide, ammonium phosphate, ammonium sulfate, ammonium sulfide) Substances made from combining ammonia with certain acids. Added to improve texture, control acidity, and sometimes to enhance flavor. Not known to be toxic. GRAS

AMMONIUM SULFATE   See sulfates

AMMONIUM SULFITE   See sulfites

ANNATTO COLOR   A yellowish vegetable dye derived from trees native to India and South America. Commonly found in cheese, sausage casings, cereal, margarine, and baked goods. Used also as a food marking ink. Not known to be toxic.

ARTIFICIAL COLOR   Coloring agents synthetically made to aid in food appearance. Usually made from coal tar (known carcinogen) derivatives such as azo, triphenylmethane and xanthene, all of which have safety questions. Some controversy exists over the connection between artificial coloring and hyperactivity in children, liver damage, and cancer. Nine artificial colors are permitted for use in foods. Two are restricted to use in single products: Citrus Red No. 2 is allowed only in the skins of oranges and is a known carcinogen; Orange B is allowed only in the casing of frankfurters and sausages. The FDA considered banning Orange B because of carcinogenic properties. The remaining seven have been the source of continued controversy. Yellow No. 5 is reported to cause allergic reactions. Other studies have been inconclusive.

ARTIFICIAL FLAVORING   The most common of all food additives. Compounds synthetically produced to copy flavors found in nature. Used in soft drinks, snacks, and many other low nutrition foods. Suspected of promoting hyperactivity in children.

ARABIC GUM   See acacia gum

ASCORBIC ACID   erythorbic acid, vitamin C (see). Commercially made through the fermentation of sorbitol. Used as a meat preservative to help maintain reddish coloring and as a dietary supplement in the form of vitamin C. Not known to be toxic. GRAS

ASCORBYL PALMITATE   The salt of ascorbic acid (see) and palmitic acid (see stearic acid). Used as a preservative in candy and soft drinks, an antioxidant to retard spoilage, a stabilizer, and an emulsifier to prevent separation. Not known to be toxic. GRAS

ASPARTAME   Known more commonly by its
brand name, NutraSweet. A compound of phenylalanine and aspartic acid. Sweetness about
200 times greater than table sugar with no
calories. Commonly found in diet drinks, cereal, soft drinks, sugar free gum, and instant tea.
The 10-year patent on aspartame expired in
1992, so expect to see it in more products and
under other brand names. Much controversy
has arisen about NutraSweet and its alleged
ability to cause brain damage, though most was
discredited by the FDA. The Mexican govern-
ment in 1988 banned the use of the prefix
"nutra," claiming it was misleading because the
product had no nutritional value. Mexico re-
quires a health warning on all products containing aspartame. Questions also exist about the
chemical changes that heat produces in aspartame. Must be avoided by sufferers of PKU.
Safety is questionable.

BAKING SODA   See sodium bicarbonate

BHA (butylated hydroxyanisole) A synthetic preservative (antioxidant) used to retard the spoilage of fats and oils. Most commonly found in chocolate, chips and pretzels, jello and pudding, instant popcorn, soft drinks, beef sticks, cake mix, icing, hard candy, soft drinks, chewing gum, cereal, frozen pies, frozen dinners, and instant tea. Known to cause allergic reactions. In 1982, a Japanese study showed it to cause cancer in lab animals. Its use in food is restricted. Many questions about its safety persist. GRAS

BHT (butylated hydroxytoluene) Similar to BHA (see), BHT is a synthetic preservative (antioxidant) used widely. Commonly found in chocolate, chips and pretzels, instant popcorn, chewing gum, cereal, beef sticks, cake mix, and frozen pies. Often added to packing material. Known to cause allergic reactions. BHT residues have been found in human fat. Its use in food is restricted. Banned in some countries. Its safety is questionable. GRAS

BENZOATE OF SODA   See benzoic acid

BENZOIC ACID (benzoate of soda, sodium benzoate)   A preservative that occurs naturally in benzoin resin and a variety of other substances. Commonly found in sugar substitutes, canned vegetables, and frozen dinners. Should be monitored by people sensitive to aspirin. Moderately toxic. Safety is questionable. GRAS

BENZOYL PEROXIDE   A bleaching agent. Commonly found in flour, some cheeses, fats, and oils. Highly toxic when inhaled. Safety is questionable. GRAS

BETA CAROTENE   Comes from colorful plants and vegetables and is converted to vitamin A in the body. Used in food as a coloring agent (orange) and a nutritional supplement. Not known to be toxic.

BICARBONATE   See carbonates

BROMINATED VEGETABLE OIL (BVO)   The
chemical bromine combined with vegetable oil
to make a stabilized oil that mixes better. Commonly found in fruit juice and soft drinks when
a citrus oil is used for flavoring. Can cause vital
organ degeneration and central nervous system
malfunctions. Removed from the GRAS list due
to potential health risks but still is being used.
Bromine is toxic when eaten and a severe skin
irritant.

BUTYLATED HYDROXYANISOLE   See BHA

BUTYLATED HYDROXYTOLUENE   See BHT

CAFFEINE   Naturally occurs in coffee, kola nuts
(cola), and tea. Added to foods as a "pick-me-
up." Stimulates the central nervous system,
increases heart rate and breathing. No evidence
of carcinogenic or mutagenic (ability to cause
genetic changes) properties. However, it has
caused birth defects in laboratory animals. Not

recommended for people with cardiovascular conditions, children, or pregnant women. However, some recent studies show moderate amounts consumed during pregnancy to be acceptable. A link between caffeine and fibrocystic breast disease has also been suggested. GRAS

CALCIFEROL   See vitamin D_2

CALCIUM ACETATE   See calcium salts

CALCIUM ALGINATE   See alginates

CALCIUM ASCORBATE   A preservative (antioxidant) made from ascorbic acid and calcium carbonate (see both). Commonly found in soft drinks and cured meat products. Not known to be toxic. GRAS

CALCIUM CARBONATE   See carbonates

CALCIUM CARRAGEENAN   See carrageenan

CALCIUM CASEINATE   See caseinates

CALCIUM CHLORIDE   See calcium salts

CALCIUM DISODIUM EDTA   A preservative that helps retain color and flavor in various foods. Also helps prevent crystallization and is used as a sequestrant to neutralize unwanted effects of metals. Found in salad dressing, prepared dips, canned vegetables, and mayonnaise. Currently being tested by the FDA for possible damage to genes and kidneys.

CALCIUM GLUCONATE   See calcium salts

CALCIUM HYDROXIDE   See calcium salts

CALCIUM IODATE   See iodine

CALCIUM OXIDE   See calcium salts

CALCIUM PEROXIDE   See calcium salts

CALCIUM PHOSPHATE (monocalcium phos-
☺ phate, dicalcium phosphate, tricalcium phosphate)   Used as a jelling ingredient, mineral
supplement, and an anticaking (to prevent lumping from moisture) ingredient respectively. Phosphates are an essential nutrient that occur naturally in dairy products, legumes, and meat. Not
known to be toxic. See phosphates. GRAS

CALCIUM PROPIONATE   See propionic acid

CALCIUM SACCHARIN   See saccharin

CALCIUM SALTS (calcium acetate, calcium chlo-
☺ ride, calcium gluconate, calcium hydroxide,
calcium oxide, calcium peroxide, calcium stearate)   These calcium salts promote good bone
development and maintenance and are vital to
other bodily functions. Used in food mainly to
add texture and balance acids. Found in bread,
soft drinks, beer, and wine. Not known to be

toxic. However, calcium peroxide is known to be a skin irritant. GRAS

CALCIUM SILICATE   Used as an anticaking ☺ agent for its moisture absorbing properties. Commonly found in table salt and baking powder. Its dust is an irritant. Not known to be toxic. GRAS

CALCIUM STEARATE   See stearic acid and calcium salts

CALCIUM SULFATE (plaster of paris)   Used as ☺ a dough conditioner and firming agent to retain crispness. Commonly found in chips and pretzels, jello and pudding, and baked goods. Not known to be toxic. GRAS

CARAMEL COLOR   See artificial colors

CARBONATES (calcium carbonate, potassium car- ☺ bonate, potassium bicarbonate, sodium bicarbonate (see))   Carbonates and bicarbonates are used primarily to neutralize acidity in foods. Also used as a leavening agent to help dough rise. Not known to be toxic. GRAS

CARBON DIOXIDE   See propellants

CARNAUBA WAX   A wax derived from a South American tree and used as a glaze, hardener, or resin. It is the hardest and most expensive wax available. Commonly found in sugar free gum and hard candy. Safety is questionable. GRAS

CAROB BEAN GUM   See locust bean gum

CAROB SEED GUM   See locust bean gum

CARRAGEENAN (calcium carrageenan)   Extracted from particular mosses, seaweeds, and red algae. Used as a stabilizer and an emulsifier to prevent separation. Commonly found in cheese foods, canned whipped cream, chocolate, and frozen desserts. Some test results show colon damage in lab animals. Safety of long-term use is questionable. GRAS

CASEINATES (ammonium caseinate, calcium caseinate, magnesium caseinate, potassium caseinate, sodium caseinate)   Casein is the main protein of milk. Used primarily as a binder, thickener, or texturizer in frozen desserts. Calcium caseinate is used as a supplement in some diet products. Should be avoided by people allergic to cow milk. Not known to be toxic. GRAS

CELLULOSE (cellulose gel, cellulose gum)   The main fiber in plants. Used as a thickener, texturizer, or stabilizer. Commonly found in mayonnaise, pancake syrup, fruit juice, brownies, and frozen pies. Not known to be toxic. GRAS

CHLOROFLUOROCARBONS
See propellants

CHOLECALCIFEROL   See vitamin D_3

CITRIC ACID   Naturally occurs in plants (citrus fruits, peaches, apricots, coffee) and animals. Commercially made through the fermentation of sugar. A multi-purpose additive used as a flavor enhancer, sequestrant to neutralize unwanted effects of metals, firming agent to retain crispness, and nutrient. Commonly found in fruit juice, beef sticks, Mexican food, mustard, cake mix, canned vegetables, baby food, and frozen pies. Not known to be toxic. GRAS

COPPER COMPOUNDS (copper carbonate, copper gluconate, copper sulfate)   Copper is an essential mineral element of most living things. Used as a nutritional supplement, stabilizer, and preservative. Commonly found in wine, sugar free gum, and baby formula. Not known to be toxic. GRAS

CORN SWEETENER (corn syrup, glucose, dextrose)   Simple sugars derived from corn that break down rapidly in the body and can cause severe fluctuations in blood sugar levels. They have no nutritional value. All fermentable sugars such as these are a major cause of tooth decay. Used in food as an alternative sweetener. Intake must be controlled by diabetics. Not known to be toxic. GRAS

COTTONSEED OIL   A vegetable oil made from the seed of a variety of cotton plants. Commonly found in chips and other snacks. Some controversy exists over the pesticides used on cotton plants. Cottonseed oil has been known to cause allergic reactions.

CREAM OF TARTAR (tartaric acid, sodium tartrate, potassium bitartrate, potassium acid tartrate)   A byproduct of wine production. Used to control acidity and as a sequestrant to neutralize unwanted effects of metals. Commonly found in sugar substitutes, wine, baking powder, and baked goods. Not known to be toxic. GRAS

CYANOCOBALAMIN   See vitamin B_{12}

CYSTEINE   An amino acid. For commercial use, made from protein or from treated cystine (see). Used as a nutritional supplement and reducing agent in dough. Commonly found in canned meat, bread, and canned fish. Not known to be toxic. GRAS

CYSTINE   A non-essential amino acid that occurs naturally in urine and hair. Made from keratin, a protein. Used in foods as a nutritional supplement. Not known to be toxic. GRAS

D-ERYTHRO-ASCORBIC ACID   See erythorbic acid

DL-A-TOCOPHEROL ACETATE   See vitamin E

7-DEHYDROCHOLESTEROL   See vitamin D_3

DEXTRIN   Produced from various starches. Used
as a thickener, sugar substitute, and stabilizer.
Commonly found in chocolate, fruit juice, sugar
free gum, and Japanese food. Intake must be
controlled by diabetics. Not known to be toxic.
GRAS

DEXTROSE   See glucose

DICALCIUM PHOSPHATE   See calcium phosphate

DIGLYCERIDES   See glycerides

DIOCTYL SODIUM SULFOSUCCINATE   A
waxy solid used as an emulsifier to prevent
separation and a dispersing agent to make ingredients dissolve better. Helps in processing of
sugar products. Commonly found in soft drinks
and products made with cocoa. Use in food is
restricted.

DIPOTASSIUM PHOSPHATE   See potassium
   phosphate

DISODIUM EDTA   See EDTA

DISODIUM GUANYLATE (sodium guanylate,
   GMP, guanylic acid)   Byproduct of disodium
   inosinate (see). Naturally occurring in all living
   cells. Found naturally in seaweed and dried
   fish. Closely related to monosodium glutamate
   (MSG). Used as flavor enhancers. They are far
   more potent than MSG, therefore can be used in
   much smaller amounts. Commonly found in
   chips and pretzels, dried fish, canned meat, and
   Japanese food. Not known to be toxic.

DISODIUM INOSINATE (IMP, inosinic acid)
   Naturally occurring in all cells. Commercially
   obtained from a derivative of yeast. Found
   naturally in seaweed and dried fish. Closely
   related to monosodium glutamate (MSG). Used
   as flavor enhancers. They are far more potent

than MSG, therefore can be used in much smaller amounts. Commonly found in chips and pretzels, dried fish, canned meat, and Japanese food. Not known to be toxic.

EDTA (ethylene diaminetetraacetic acid, calcium disodium EDTA)   Used as a preservative and a sequestrant to neutralize unwanted effects of metals. Commonly found in canned vegetables, cheese foods, fruit drinks, mayonnaise, and beer. These salts have proven to be highly effective when used as preservatives. On a list of chemicals to be studied for possible reproductive hazards. Not known to be toxic. GRAS

ENZYMES   A protein used to start many biochemical reactions. See rennet

ERGOCALCIFEROL   See vitamin D_2

ERYTHORBIC ACID (isoascorbic acid, d-erythro-ascorbic acid)   Used as a preservative, closely related to ascorbic acid. Also acts as a color fixative, and in brewing, an antioxidant to retard spoilage. Commonly found in soft drinks. Not known to be toxic. GRAS

ETHOXYLATED MONO- AND DIGLYCERIDE
See glycerides

ETHYL CITRATE   See triethyl citrate

ETHYLENE DIAMINETETRAACETIC ACID
See EDTA

FD&C COLORS   Synthetic colors used in food, drugs, and cosmetics. See artificial colors

FERROUS GLUCONATE   Used as a coloring and flavoring agent, also as a source of iron. Commonly found in pickled items, cereal, and black olives. One study showed use on the skin of lab mice caused tumors. However, not proven to be toxic when eaten. GRAS

FERROUS SULFATE   Added to food as a source of iron. Commercially obtained through treated steel. Commonly found in baby food. Recent studies suggest a link between elevated levels of iron and heart disease. Can cause intestinal problems. GRAS

FOLIC ACID   A member of the vitamin B (see) family. Essential to healthy tissue growth. Used as a nutrient. Commonly found in fruit juice and cereal. Not known to be toxic.

FRUCTOSE (fruit sugar)   A simple carbohydrate found naturally in many fruits and honey. Converted to glucose in the body for energy. Commonly found in pancake syrup, fruit juice, steak sauce, and honey. As with any fermentable sugar, tooth decay should be a concern. Intake must be controlled by diabetics. Not known to be toxic.

FRUIT SUGAR   See fructose

FUMARIC ACID   Naturally occurs in most living things. Manufactured synthetically. Used as a preservative, flavor enhancer, an acidulant to fight bacteria, and often as a substitute for cream of tartar (see). Commonly found in sugar substitutes, jello, pudding, and fruit juice. Not known to be toxic. GRAS

GELATIN   The main protein found in animal tissue. Derived for commercial use from beef and pork skin, ligaments, and tendons. Used as a thickener in pudding and gelatin desserts. Not known to be toxic.

GLUCOSE (dextrose)   A simple sugar made mostly from corn and grapes. Occurs naturally in plants and also in blood. Other sugars are converted to glucose for use in the body. Made for commercial use by combining corn starch with enzymes and acids. Sweeter than table sugar (sucrose). Commonly found in chocolate, sugar substitutes, chips and pretzels, beef sticks, cereal, hard candy, and fruit juice. As with any fermentable sugar, tooth decay should be a concern. Intake must be monitored by diabetics. Not known to be toxic.

GLYCERIDES (ethoxylated, succinylated, mono-, di- and triglycerides) Commonly, mono-, di-, and triglycerides. Components of fatty acids chemically combined with glycerol (see), an alcohol. They are used as emulsifiers to prevent separation, crystallization inhibitors, and preservatives. They are handled by the body as fat and may increase the calorie and cholesterol content of food. Commonly found in chips and pretzels, soft drinks, shortening, seasoning mix, cake mix, hard candy, cupcakes, and bread. Not known to be toxic. GRAS

GLYCERIN   See glycerol

GLYCEROL (glycerin)   An alcohol naturally found in all fats. Most commonly made from a byproduct of soap or synthesized chemically. It's used as a humectant to retain moisture, texturizer, and plasticizer to add flexibility. Commonly found in sugar free gum, toothpaste, cereal, hard candy, meat, and marshmallows. Not known to be toxic. GRAS

GMP   See disodium guanylate

GUANYLIC ACID   See disodium guanylate

GUAR GUM   A vegetable gum made from the seed of the guar plant, found in Pakistan and India. Used as a stabilizer, emulsifier to prevent separation, and thickener. Commonly found in pickled items, frozen dinners, soft drinks, cheese, Mexican food, cereal, and frozen whipped cream. Higher doses may cause intestinal problems. GRAS

GUM ARABIC   See acacia gum

HEXANEDIOIC ACID   See adipic acid

HIGH FRUCTOSE CORN SYRUP   A corn
sweetener (see) treated with an enzyme to make
it sweeter. Has no nutritional value other than
calories. Commonly found in soft drinks. All
fermentable sugars such as these are a major
cause of tooth decay. Used in food as an alternative sweetener. Not known to be toxic. GRAS

HYDROGENATED VEGETABLE OIL   Par-
tially solidified vegetable oils. Made from the
reaction of hydrogen with vegetable oils. Commonly found in chocolate, icing, and Mexican
food. Some studies suggest a link to colon
cancer. Safety is questionable.

HYDROLYZED VEGETABLE PROTEIN (HVP,
hydrolyzed plant protein (soy), hydrolyzed protein)   Plant protein chemically treated to act as

a flavor enhancer. Often contains MSG. Commonly found in chips and pretzels, canned fish, soup, hot dogs, and Japanese food. GRAS

IMP   See disodium inosinate

INOSINIC ACID   See disodium inosinate

INOSITOL   A member of the vitamin B (see) family. Occurs naturally in plant and animal tissue. Used in food as a nutrient. Not known to be toxic. GRAS

INVERT SUGAR   A blend of glucose (50%) and fructose (50%) sugars. Sweeter and more soluble than table sugar, making it a common ingredient in syrup. As with any fermentable sugar, tooth decay should be a concern. Not known to be toxic. GRAS

IODINE (calcium iodate, potassium iodate, potassium iodide)   Occurs naturally in most shellfish and sometimes drinking water. Commercially obtained from salt water or kelp. An essential part of a healthy diet. Used in food as a nutrient. Extremely low toxicity in appropriate quantities, but highly toxic in larger doses. Has been known to cause allergic reactions in susceptible people.

IRON   An essential mineral found abundantly in nature. Added to food to regain nutritional value lost in processing. Organ meats are a good source of iron. Recent studies suggest a link between higher levels of iron and heart disease. See ferrous sulfate. GRAS

ISOASCORBIC ACID   See erythorbic acid

ISOLEUCINE   See amino acids

LACTIC ACID   A product of energy production (metabolism) in the body. Found in almost every living thing. Commercially obtained through the fermentation of starch, milk whey, potatoes, and molasses. Used to inhibit spoilage, control acidity and, in some cases, to add tartness. Commonly found in chips and pretzels, Mexican food, and Japanese food. Not known to be toxic. GRAS

LACTOSE (milk sugar)   Occurs naturally in milk and dairy products. Some people have a low tolerance to lactose, but it is considered safe. Not known to be toxic. GRAS

LECITHIN   Natural constituent of plants and animals. A natural byproduct of soybean oil (its cheapest source). Other commercial sources include corn, seeds, egg yolk, and animals. Lecithin is a good source of choline, which is important for liver function. Used as an emulsifier to prevent separation and antioxidant to retard spoilage. Commonly found in seasoning mix, cake mix, cereal, hard candy, soft drinks, frozen dinners, cupcakes, and margarine. Not known to be toxic. GRAS

LEUCINE See amino acids

LOCUST BEAN GUM (carob bean gum, carob seed gum, St. John's Bread) A vegetable gum that comes from the seed of the carob tree. Used as a stabilizer and texturizer. Commonly found in frozen dinners and cereal. Some questions about the safety of vegetable gums exist. GRAS

LYSINE See amino acids

MAGNESIUM CASEINATE See caseinates

MAGNESIUM COMPOUNDS (magnesium acetate, magnesium carbonate, magnesium chloride, magnesium hydroxide, magnesium oxide, magnesium phosphate, magnesium stearate, magnesium sulfate, magnesium silicate) Magnesium is an essential part of the diet and can be found in its variations listed above. They are found readily in nature and processed for use as additives. Used as firming agents to retain crispness, anticaking agents to prevent lumping from moisture, flavor enhancers, and nutrients. Also used as alkalis to control acidity. All magnesium compounds are considered nontoxic☺ except: magnesium silicate ☹which is toxic by inhalation and has been linked to kidney damage, magnesium chloride ☺ which is toxic when eaten, magnesium oxide☹which is toxic by inhalation. GRAS

MALIC ACID   Occurs naturally in most vegetables and fruits, particularly unripe apples. Made synthetically for commercial use. Used in food as an acidifier to add tartness, and as a flavoring agent often found in wine. Commonly used in fruit juice, soft drinks, wine, cereal, and frozen pies. Not known to be toxic. GRAS

MALT EXTRACT (malt flavoring)   Extracted from barley and used as a flavoring agent and nutrient. Commonly found in cereal and beer. Not known to be toxic. GRAS

MALT FLAVORING   See malt extract

MALTODEXTRIN   A sugar that comes from starch. Used as a texturizer and flavor enhancer. Commonly found in chips and pretzels, sugar substitutes, Mexican food, cereal, and soft drinks. Not known to be toxic. GRAS

MANNITOL   A sugar that occurs naturally in a variety of vegetables and seaweeds. For use as an additive, it is produced by adding hydrogen to corn sugar (glucose). Commonly used in sugar free gum, although it does contain calories and is considered a carbohydrate. Found also as a "dusting" on sticks of gum. It also can act as a texturizer in many foods. In higher doses it may have a laxative effect. Otherwise, not known to be toxic. GRAS

MENADIONE   See vitamin K_3

MENAQUINONE   See vitamin K_2

METHIONINE   See amino acids

METHYLPARABEN   See parabens

MILK SUGAR   See lactose

MODIFIED FOOD STARCH   Starch that has
☹ been chemically modified for various reasons
such as ease of digestion for infants. Commonly
found in baby food, Mexican food, and steak
sauce. Further testing is necessary to determine
safety.

MONOGLYCERIDES   See glycerides

MONOCALCIUM PHOSPHATE   See calcium
phosphate

MONOPOTASSIUM PHOSPHATE   See potassium phosphate

MONOSODIUM GLUTAMATE (MSG)   The sodium salt of glutamic acid, an amino acid that helps to form protein. Found naturally in seaweed and soybeans. MSG is commercially made by the bacterial fermentation of sugar. Can produce "Chinese Restaurant Syndrome", a term coined to describe the physical reaction to MSG. Symptoms include mood swings, rashes, itching, burning sensations, tightness in chest, breathing difficulties, asthma, depression, anxiety, and headaches. Not recommended for pregnant women. Destroyed brain cells of infant lab animals, including those of a monkey. Sensitivity to MSG can vary dramatically from person to person. Commonly found in salad dressing, canned meat, canned fish, chips and pretzels, fruit juice, Mexican food, Japanese food, baby formula, and frozen dinners. Further studies needed to determine safety. GRAS

NIACIN (niacinamide, nicotinic acid)   A member
☺ of the vitamin B (see) family, essential for the
maintenance of a healthy nervous system and
the prevention of the disease pellagra. Used as
a nutritional supplement. Commonly found in
enriched flour and cereal. Niacin is known to be
toxic at higher levels, causing flushing, nausea,
vomiting, headaches, and skin lesions. GRAS

NIACINAMIDE   See niacin

NICOTINIC ACID   See niacin

NITRATE (potassium nitrate, sodium nitrate, so-
☹ dium nitrite)   Nitrate and nitrite are closely
related chemically. They have been used to
preserve color in packaged, cured meats. A
secondary benefit is their ability to prevent the
growth of bacteria that causes botulism. These
additives have been heavily linked to cancer in
laboratory experiments.   Nitrite, when combined with stomach fluid, creates a powerful

carcinogen called nitrosamine. Despite their safety risks, nitrate and nitrite are very effective as food additives. Commonly found in cured meats and vegetables that have been treated with nitrogen-based fertilizers. They should be avoided, especially by pregnant women and children. Vitamin C was found to help offset the ill effects of nitrates.

NITRITE   See nitrate

NITROUS OXIDE (laughing gas)   A propellant for whipped cream. Also used as an anesthetic, most commonly by dentists. Nontoxic when used as a propellant. See propellants. GRAS

NUTRASWEET   See aspartame

OLESTRA   A fat substitute made from sucrose and edible fats and oils. It has no calories and is virtually unabsorbed by the body. Its maker,

Procter & Gamble, has asked for FDA approval to use olestra. May be found in home cooking oils and shortenings. Also may be used for deep-fried snacks such as chips and corn puffs.

PALM OIL   Made from a particular palm tree. Often used as a substitute for tallow. Commonly found in jello and pudding. Tropical oils are known to be high in saturated fat.

PALMITIC ACID   See stearic acid

PARABENS (methylparaben, propylparaben)   Synthetic substances produced as mold-inhibiting preservatives. Closely related to sodium benzoate. Commonly found in baked goods and sugar substitutes. Propylparaben ☺ has shown no signs of toxicity. Methylparaben☺ has caused birth defects when fed to pregnant lab animals. GRAS

PECTIN   Found naturally in nearly all plants as a carbohydrate that helps in cell formation. Used as a stabilizer and thickener. Commonly found in icing, cereal, fruit juice, soft drinks, jelly, and preserves. Natural pectin in fruit used for jelly usually breaks down in processing, so purified pectin is added to help the process. Not known to be toxic. GRAS

PHENYLALANINE An amino acid (see). Essential for normal growth. Not synthesized by the body, therefore must be obtained through diet. Those who suffer from phenylketonuria (PKU) must avoid phenylalanine. Nontoxic for others.

PHOSPHATES (ammonium phosphate, calcium phosphate (see), tricalcium phosphate, potassium phosphate (see), dipotassium phosphate, sodium phosphate, trisodium phosphate; phosphoric acid, sodium hexametaphosphate (see), sodium pyrophosphate) Used in food as a texturizer, flavoring agent, nutritional supplement, sequestrant to neutralize unwanted effects of metals, and an alkali to remove excess acid. Phosphates are an important nutrient in a healthy diet. When eaten at high levels, phosphates are toxic and may cause kidney malfunction and contribute to osteoporosis—particularly phosphoric acid☹. Otherwise not known to be toxic. GRAS

PHOSPHORIC ACID   See phosphates

PHYLLOQUININE   See vitamin K$_1$

PLASTER OF PARIS   See calcium sulfate

POLYSORBATE 60 & POLYSORBATE 80
☺ Created by combining sorbitol (see) with certain fatty acids. Used to prevent separation as an emulsifier and a stabilizer. Commonly found in salad dressings, brownies, frozen dessert toppings, cupcakes, and pickled items. Not known to be toxic.

POTASSIUM ALGINATE   See alginates

POTASSIUM BICARBONATE   See carbonates

POTASSIUM BISULFITE   See sulfites

POTASSIUM BITARTRATE   See cream of tartar

POTASSIUM BROMATE   Added to flour to
☹ improve texture in finished products. Commonly found in rolls, bread, and pasta. Pro-
moted renal cancer in lab animals and is al-
ready banned in some countries. Strong irritant;
use is regulated. GRAS

POTASSIUM CASEINATE   See caseinates

POTASSIUM CARBONATE   See carbonates

POTASSIUM CHLORIDE   A potassium salt.
☺ Used to promote fermentation in brewing. Commercially obtained through the processing of
salt water. Commonly found in brewed products and jelly. Not known to be toxic. GRAS

POTASSIUM CITRATE ☺ Used as a buffer to balance acidity in artificially sweetened jams. Also found in fruit juice. Not known to be toxic. GRAS

POTASSIUM IODATE See iodine

POTASSIUM IODIDE See iodine

POTASSIUM METABISULFITE See sulfites

POTASSIUM NITRATE See nitrate

POTASSIUM PHOSPHATE (monopotassium ☺ phosphate, dipotassium phosphate) Made from the reaction of phosphoric acid and calcium carbonate (see carbonates). Used in food as a buffer to balance acidity, sequestrant to neutralize unwanted effects of metals, and a yeast food for brewing. Commonly found in beer, champagne, wine, and baked goods. See also phosphates. Not known to be toxic.

POTASSIUM PYROSULFITE   See sulfites

POTASSIUM SORBATE   The potassium salt of
sorbic acid (see). Used as a preservative and
mold inhibitor. Commonly found in salad dressing, steak sauce, Japanese food, processed meat,
sausage, soft drinks, wine, icing, and margarine. Toxicity is very low. GRAS

POTASSIUM SULFATE   See sulfates

POTASSIUM SULFITE   See sulfites

PROPELLANTS (carbon dioxide, chlorofluorocarbons, nitrous oxide) Gases used to dispense
contents from aerosol containers. Chlorofluorocarbons are rarely used by manufacturers due
to their link to the depletion of the ozone layer.
Nitrous oxide is used in whipped cream canis-
ters. Carbon dioxide gives bubbles to sodas.
Nontoxic when used as propellants.

PROPIONIC ACID (calcium propionate, sodium propionate)   Found naturally in Swiss cheese and other dairy products, fruit, and vegetables. Used as a mold inhibitor in bread and cheese. Strong irritant. Not known to be toxic. GRAS

PROPYL GALLATE   Used as an antioxidant to retard spoilage. Often combined with BHA and BHT. Commonly found in frozen pies, items that contain animal fat or other oils, and chewing gum. Long-term studies suggest it is a possible carcinogen, though it is not proven. Use in food is restricted to .02% of the fat content of the product. Not known to be toxic. GRAS

PROPYLENE GLYCOL (propylene glycol monostearate, propylene alginate)   Made from a petroleum byproduct and from glycerol (see glycerin). Used as a humectant to retain moisture. Commonly found in jello and pudding, salad dressing, brownies, and baked goods. Not known to be toxic. GRAS

PROPYLENE GLYCOL ALGINATE
See propylene glycol and alginates

PROPYLPARABEN   See parabens

PSYLLIUM   Made from the seed of the fleawort
☺ plant. Used in food as a stabilizer. Commonly
found in diet drinks and frozen desserts. Not
known to be toxic.

PYRIDOXINE (pyridoxine hydrochloride)
See vitamin B_6

PYROPHOSPHATE   See phosphates and sodium
acid pyrophosphate

QUININE (quinine hydrochloride, quinine sulfate)
☹ Comes from the bark of a South American tree.
First discovered as a cure for malaria in the
1600s. Used currently as a flavoring agent,
usually in tonics. Some evidence shows that
quinine can cause birth defects. Long-term use

is thought to impair hearing and in concentrated form can affect vision. Quinine should be avoided by pregnant women and hypersensitive people.

RENNET (rennin, enzymes)   A stomach enzyme that causes milk to curdle and can coagulate 25,000 times its own weight of milk. Made commercially from the inner stomach linings of calves. Enzymes, when added to milk, create cheese. Not known to be toxic. GRAS

RIBOFLAVIN   See vitamin B_2

SACCHARIN (sodium saccharin, calcium saccharin)   An artificial sweetener 400 times as sweet as table sugar (sucrose). Discovered in the late 1800s from a coal tar derivative. It is a non-caloric, non-nutritive sweetener. Commonly found in sugar free gum, soft drinks, instant tea, and sugar substitutes. Saccharin has been widely replaced by NutraSweet after saccharin was found to cause cancerous tumors in the bladders of lab animals. Saccharin presents a health risk at very high doses.

ST. JOHN'S BREAD   See locust bean gum

SALT   See sodium chloride

SILICON DIOXIDE   A substance that occurs abundantly in nature. Used as an anticaking agent to prevent lumping from moisture. Commonly found in sugar substitutes and seasoning mix. Not known to be toxic. GRAS

SIMPLESSE®   A fat substitute made from the proteins of milk and egg. Commonly found in ice cream and butter substitutes. Relatively new on the market, Simplesse should start appearing in more products. Safety may be questionable. GRAS

SMOKE FLAVORING   Made from wood smoke
condensation. Commonly found in beef sticks
and barbecue sauce. Safety is questionable.

SODA ASH   See sodium carbonate

SODIUM ACID PYROPHOSPHATE (SAP)
Used in self-rising flours as a buffer to balance
acidity. Also used as a color enhancer and
fixative. Commonly found in chips and pretzels, cake mix, and icing. Not known to be
toxic. GRAS

SODIUM ALGINATE   See alginates

SODIUM ALUMINUM PHOSPHATE   Used in
self-rising flours as a buffer to balance acidity.
Not known to be toxic. GRAS

SODIUM ASCORBATE   See vitamin C

SODIUM BENZOATE   See benzoic acid

SODIUM BICARBONATE (baking soda)   Used in all leavened products. Baking soda produces a gas that expands the dough when combined with certain acids. May affect the toxicity of certain medications. Not known to be toxic. GRAS

SODIUM BISULFATE   See sulfates

SODIUM BISULFITE   See sulfites

SODIUM CARBONATE (soda ash)   Found abundantly in nature. Used in foods as an alkali to remove excess acid. Commonly found in frozen dinners. Not known to be toxic. GRAS

SODIUM CASEINATE   See caseinates

SODIUM CHLORIDE (table salt)   Found abundantly in nature. Used in foods as a seasoning, curing agent, nutritional supplement, preservative for cured meats, and pickling agent. Salt

poses a health risk for those who have a tendency toward high blood pressure. Not known
to be toxic. GRAS

SODIUM CITRATE   Used to control acidity.
Commonly found in jello and pudding, fruit
juice, and soft drinks. Can alter the toxicity of
certain medications. Recent studies suggest citrates can enhance the ill-effects of aluminum
compounds (see). GRAS

SODIUM DIACETATE   Made from the combination of acetic acid (see) and sodium acetate, the
salt of acetic acid. Used as a mold inhibitor and
a buffer to balance acidity. Commonly found in
baked goods, chips, and pretzels. Not known to
be toxic. GRAS

SODIUM ERYTHORBATE   Similar to vitamin C
(see), however sodium erythorbate is non-nutri-
tional. Used as an antioxidant to retard spoilage
and a color fixative. Commonly found in beef

sticks and baked goods. Not known to be toxic. GRAS

SODIUM GUANYLATE   See disodium guanylate

SODIUM HEXAMETAPHOSPHATE   Used as a sequestrant to neutralize unwanted effects of metals, an emulsifier to prevent separation, an antioxidant to retard spoilage, and a texturizer. Commonly found in pancake syrup, cereal, frozen whipped cream, and ice cream. See phosphates. Not known to be toxic. GRAS

SODIUM LAURYL SULFATE   Made from the combination of a derivative of fatty oils and sulfuric acid. Used as an emulsifier to prevent separation and an aid in whipping. Commonly found in toothpaste, cake mix, and candy. Not known to be toxic. GRAS

SODIUM METABISULFITE   See sulfites

SODIUM NITRATE   See nitrate

SODIUM NITRITE   See nitrate

SODIUM PHOSPHATE   See phosphates

SODIUM PROPIONATE   See propionic acid

SODIUM PYROPHOSPHATE   See phosphates

SODIUM SACCHARIN   See saccharin

SODIUM SILICO ALUMINATE   Used in sodium chloride (table salt) as an anticaking agent to prevent lumping from moisture. Not known to be toxic. GRAS

SODIUM STEARATE   A fatty acid made from vegetable oils and animal fats. Used as an emulsifier to prevent separation. Not known to be toxic. GRAS

SODIUM STEAROYL-2-LACTYLATE Made from the combination of lactic acid (see) and fatty acids from vegetable oils or animal fats. Used in food as an emulsifier to prevent separation. Commonly found in chips and pretzels, frozen dinners, frozen desserts, rolls, and bread. Not known to be toxic.

SODIUM SULFITE See sulfites

SODIUM TARTRATE See cream of tartar

SODIUM TRIPOLYPHOSPHATE (STP) Used in curing solutions for packaged meats, and as a sequestrant to neutralize unwanted effects of metals and an antioxidant to retard spoilage. Commonly found in canned meats and alcoholic beverages. Not known to be toxic. GRAS

SORBIC ACID (acetic acid (see), potassium sorbate) Obtained naturally from the berries of the mountain ash (rowanberry tree) and is also synthesized chemically. Used as a mold and bacteria inhibitor. Commonly found in pancake syrup, cheese foods, and cupcakes. Not known to be toxic. GRAS

SORBITAN MONOSTEARATE   Used as an emulsifier to prevent separation. Commonly found in chocolate, frozen whipped cream, and cupcakes. Not known to be toxic.

SORBITOL   A sweet alcohol made from the combination of glucose (corn sugar) and hydrogen. It is a multi-purpose ingredient used as a humectant to retain moisture, stabilizer, and sugar substitute. It is about half as sweet as table sugar (sucrose) and breaks down very slowly in the body, therefore avoiding high blood sugar levels. Commonly found in chocolate, sugar free gum, toothpaste, and cereal. Large doses may have a laxative effect. Not known to be toxic.

STEARIC ACID (palmitic acid, octadecanoic acid)
☺ A saturated fatty acid found naturally in many oils. Used in food as a texturizer. Commonly found in chewing gum, soft drinks, and baked goods. Not known to be toxic. GRAS

SUCCINIC ACID   Occurs naturally in fungi,
☺ meat, cheese, and vegetables. Used as a neutralizer to adjust acidity. Commonly found in Japanese food. Not known to be toxic. GRAS

SUCCINYLATED MONOGLYCERIDES
See glycerides

SUCROSE (table sugar)   Found in all plants. Made
☹ commercially from sugar cane, it is stripped of most vitamins, minerals, and proteins during processing. Sucrose is comprised of fructose and glucose. Americans eat 65 to 120 lbs. per person yearly. Sucrose and other fermentable sugars are the number one cause of tooth decay. Diabetics must monitor their intake of sucrose. Not known to be toxic. GRAS

SUGAR   See sucrose

SULFATES (sulfuric acid, ammonium sulfate, calcium sulfate (see), potassium sulfate, sodium
sulfate, sodium bisulfate)   Known as sulfates
when used with food. Sulfates are multi-purpose. They can act as firming agents to retain
crispness, acidifiers and alkalis to balance acidity, and nutritional supplements. Commonly
found in baked products, cereal, and tomato-
based products. Nontoxic at current levels in
food. However, high concentrations of sulfuric
acid can severely damage skin and be fatal
when eaten. GRAS

SULFITES (potassium bisulfite, sodium bisulfite,
potassium metabisulfite, sodium metabisulfite,
sodium sulfite, sodium bisulfite, potassium
sulfite, ammonium sulfite, potassium pyrosulfite,
sulphur dioxide)   Used as antioxidants and
preservatives to retard spoilage, and in wine to
kill undesirable bacteria. They also inhibit

discoloration. Commonly found in ketchup, canned fish, chips and pretzels, dried fruit, pie filling, seasoning mix, Japanese food, cereal, wine, beer, hard candy, and frozen dinners. Many questions about their safety exist. Several deaths have been attributed to sulfites. They are also known to cause severe reactions in asthmatics. Not permitted in meat or other food that contains thiamine (vitamin B_1) because of their ability to break down the vitamin.

SULFUR DIOXIDE   See sulfites

SULFURIC ACID   See sulfates

SULPHUR DIOXIDE   See sulfites

SUNETTE   See acesulfame potassium

TBHQ (tertiary butylhydroquinone)   Similar to BHA (see). Used as an antioxidant to retard spoilage. Commonly found in chips and pretzels, chocolate, jello and pudding, seasoning mix, Japanese food, icing, and hard candy. Its safety is questionable. GRAS

TARTARIC ACID   See cream of tartar

TAURINE   An amino acid vital to the development of healthy tissue. Occurs in high concentrations in milk. Commonly found in baby formula. Not known to be toxic.

TERTIARY BUTYLHYDROQUINONE
See TBHQ

TETRAPOTASSIUM PHOSPHATE
See tetrasodium pyrophosphate

TETRASODIUM PYROPHOSPHATE
(tetrapotassium phosphate)   Used as an emulsifier to prevent separation and a sequestrant to neutralize unwanted effects of metals. Commonly found in ice cream and cheese. Not

known to be toxic. GRAS when used for pack-
aging.

THIAMINE   See vitamin B_1

THIAMINE MONONITRATE (thiamine nitrate,
☺ thiamine hydrochloride)   Synthetically produced vitamin B_1 (see). Used as a dietary supplement. Commonly found in cereal, cake mix,
and cupcakes. Not known to be toxic. GRAS

THREONINE   See amino acids

TOCOPHEROLS   See vitamin E

TRICALCIUM PHOSPHATE   See phosphates

TRIETHYL CITRATE (ethyl citrate)   Made from
☺ citric acid which naturally occurs in plants
(citrus fruits, peaches, apricots, coffee) and animals. A multi-purpose additive used as a flavor
enhancer, sequestrant to neutralize unwanted

effects of metals, and preservative. Commonly found in fruit juice, beef sticks, Mexican food, mustard, cake mix, canned vegetables, baby food, and frozen pies. Use restricted to no more than .25% in a food item. Not known to be toxic. GRAS

TRIGLYCERIDES   See glycerides

TRISODIUM PHOSPHATE   See phosphates

TRYPTOPHAN   See amino acids

TUMERIC   An herb. Used as a flavoring and coloring agent. Commonly found in pickled items, mustard, and frozen dinners. Not known to be toxic. GRAS

VALINE   See amino acids

VANILLIN   Synthetic vanilla flavoring or extract. A combination of vanilla extract and ethyl vanillin.

Commonly found in chocolate, baked goods, and hard candy. Not known to be toxic. GRAS

VITAMIN A (vitamin A acetate, vitamin A palmitate, DL-A-tocopherol acetate)   Good sources include dairy products, seafood, and organ meats. Essential for good eyesight and bone development. Used as a nutritional supplement. Toxic at higher levels. Intake should be monitored. GRAS

VITAMIN B₁ (thiamine)   Good sources include vegetables, organ meats, and grains. Essential to good health. Necessary for healthy tissue and food-to-energy conversion (metabolism). Used as a nutritional supplement. Commonly found in cereal, enriched flour, and baked products. Not known to be toxic. GRAS

VITAMIN B₂ (riboflavin)   Good sources include vegetables, organ meats, and grains. Aids in metabolism (converting food into energy).

Essential to healthy skin and hair and cell maintenance. Used as a coloring agent and a nutritional supplement. Commonly found in cereal, cake mix, bread, and pasta. Not known to be toxic. GRAS

VITAMIN B$_6$ (pyridoxine, pyridoxine hydrochloride)   Good sources include vegetables, organ meats, and grains. Aids in metabolism (converting food into energy) and development of hemoglobin in red blood cells. Used as a nutritional supplement. Commonly found in cereal, cake mix, bread, and pasta. Not known to be toxic. GRAS

VITAMIN B$_{12}$ (cyanocobalamin)   Good source is organ meats. Aids in metabolism (converting food into energy). Essential to cell maintenance. Added to foods as a nutritional supplement. Commonly found in cereal, cake mix, bread, and pasta. Not known to be toxic. GRAS

VITAMIN C (ascorbic acid, sodium ascorbate)   Good sources include citrus fruit and juice. Versatile food additive. Essential to a healthy diet. Used primarily as a preservative (antioxidant) and nutritional supplement. Commonly found in soft drinks, juice, canned vegetables, baby formula, and frozen pies. Known to cause kidney stones at higher levels. GRAS

VITAMIN D₂ (ergocalciferol, calciferol)   Good sources include organ meats and fish oils. Necessary for the utilization of calcium and general bone health. Used in food as a nutritional supplement. Commonly found in milk and baby food. Toxic at high levels. Intake should be monitored. GRAS

VITAMIN D₃ (cholecalciferol, 7-dehydrocholesterol) Good sources include organ meats and fish oils. Necessary for the use of calcium and general bone health. Used as a nutritional supplement. Commonly found in milk and baby food. Toxic at high levels. Intake should be monitored. GRAS

VITAMIN E (tocopherols)   Occurs naturally in plants and animals. Commercially produced by modifying vegetable oils or, most often, by synthesis. Essential to healthy muscle development and cell formation. Used as a preservative (antioxidant) and a nutritional supplement. Toxic at high levels over long periods of time. Intake should be monitored. GRAS

VITAMIN K$_1$ (phylloquinine)   Found naturally in leafy green vegetables. Helps blood to clot. A normal adult diet supplies enough vitamin K$_1$. Use in food is limited to infant formula and baby food as a nutritional supplement. Not known to be toxic.

VITAMIN K$_2$ (menaquinone)   Produced naturally from bacteria. Helps the blood to clot. A normal adult diet supplies enough vitamin K$_2$. Use in food is limited to infant formula and baby food as a nutritional supplement. Not known to be toxic.

VITAMIN K$_3$ (menadione) Produced synthetically. ☹ Helps the blood to clot. A normal adult diet supplies enough vitamin K$_3$. Use in food is limited to infant formula and baby food as a nutritional supplement. The body absorbs vitamin K$_3$ more easily than vitamins K$_1$ and K$_2$. Known to be toxic at higher levels, causing hemolytic anemia, hyperbilirubinemia, and death.

WHEY SOLIDS The residue that is produced ☺ when casein (see) is removed from milk. It is used to make cheese. Not known to be toxic. GRAS

XANTHAN GUM A complex carbohydrate gum ☺ made from the fermentation of carbohydrates by a microorganism. Used as a stabilizer, thickener, and emulsifier to prevent separation. Commonly found in salad dressing, frozen dinners, Mexican food, and frozen whipped cream. Not known to be toxic. GRAS

XYLITOL   Made from byproducts of wood. A sugar alcohol used as a sugar substitute. Commonly found in sugar free gum. Safety is questionable. It is a possible carcinogen.

Safety Ratings at a Glance

ACACIA GUM

ADENOSINE 5

ADIPIC ACID

AMINO ACIDS

AMMONIUM BICARBONATE

AMMONIUM CARBONATE

AMMONIUM CASEINATE

AMMONIUM CHLORIDE

AMMONIUM HYDROXIDE

AMMONIUM PHOSPHATE

AMMONIUM SULFIDE

ANNATTO COLOR

ASCORBIC ACID

ASCORBYL PALMITATE

BAKING SODA

BETA CAROTENE

CALCIFEROL

CALCIUM ACETATE

CALCIUM ASCORBATE

CALCIUM CARBONATE

CALCIUM CASEINATE

CALCIUM CHLORIDE

CALCIUM GLUCONATE

CALCIUM HYDROXIDE

CALCIUM IODATE

CALCIUM OXIDE

CALCIUM PEROXIDE

CALCIUM PHOSPHATE

CALCIUM PROPIONATE

CALCIUM SILICATE

CALCIUM STEARATE

CALCIUM SULFATE

CARBON DIOXIDE

CELLULOSE

CELLULOSE GEL

CELLULOSE GUM

CHLOROFLUOROCARBONS

CHOLECALCIFEROL

CITRIC ACID

CREAM OF TARTAR

CYANOCOBALAMIN

CYSTEINE

CYSTINE

D-ERYTHRO-ASCORBIC ACID

DL-A-TOCOPHEROL ACETATE

7-DEHYDROCHOLESTEROL

DEXTRIN

DICALCIUM PHOSPHATE

DIGLYCERIDES

DIPOTASSIUM PHOSPHATE

DISODIUM GUANYLATE

DISODIUM INOSINATE

EDTA

ENZYMES

ERGOCALCIFEROL

ERYTHORBIC ACID

ETHOXYLATED GLYCERIDES

ETHYL CITRATE

ETHYLENE DIAMINETETRAACETIC ACID

FOLIC ACID

FUMARIC ACID

GELATIN

GLYCERIN

GLYCEROL

GMP

GUANYLIC ACID

GUM ARABIC

HEXANEDIOIC ACID

HVP

HYDROLYZED PLANT PROTEIN

HYDROLYZED PROTEIN

HYDROLYZED VEGETABLE PROTEIN

IMP

INOSINIC ACID

INOSITOL

IODINE

ISOASCORBIC ACID

LACTIC ACID

LACTOSE

LECITHIN

MAGNESIUM ACETATE

MAGNESIUM CARBONATE

MAGNESIUM CASEINATE

MAGNESIUM HYDROXIDE

MAGNESIUM PHOSPHATE

MAGNESIUM STEARATE

MAGNESIUM SULFATE

MALIC ACID

MALT EXTRACT

MALT FLAVORING

MALTODEXTRIN

MANNITOL

MENAQUINONE

MONOCALCIUM PHOSPHATE

MONOGLYCERIDES

MONOPOTASSIUM PHOSPHATE

NITROUS OXIDE

PECTIN

PHENYLALANINE

PHYLLOQUININE

PLASTER OF PARIS

POLYSORBATE 60

POLYSORBATE 80

POTASSIUM ACID TARTRATE

POTASSIUM BICARBONATE

POTASSIUM BITARTRATE

POTASSIUM CARBONATE

POTASSIUM CASEINATE

POTASSIUM CHLORIDE

POTASSIUM CITRATE

POTASSIUM IODATE

POTASSIUM IODIDE

POTASSIUM PHOSPHATE

POTASSIUM SORBATE

PROPIONIC ACID

PROPYLENE ALGINATE

PROPYLENE GLYCOL

PROPYLENE GLYCOL MONOSTEARATE

PSYLLIUM

PYRIDOXINE

PYRIDOXINE HYDROCHLORIDE

RENNET

RENNIN

RIBOFLAVIN

SAP

SILICON DIOXIDE

SODA ASH

SODIUM ACID PYROPHOSPHATE

SODIUM ALUMINUM PHOSPHATE

SODIUM ASCORBATE

SODIUM BICARBONATE

SODIUM CARBONATE

SODIUM CASEINATE

SODIUM CITRATE

SODIUM DIACETATE

SODIUM ERYTHORBATE

SODIUM GUANYLATE

SODIUM HEXAMETAPHOSPHATE

SODIUM LAURYL SULFATE

SODIUM PHOSPHATE

SODIUM PROPIONATE

SODIUM PYROPHOSPHATE

SODIUM SILICO ALUMINATE

SODIUM STEARATE

SODIUM STEAROYL-2-LACTYLATE

SODIUM TARTRATE

SODIUM TRIPOLYPHOSPHATE

SORBIC ACID

SORBITAN MONOSTEARATE

SORBITOL

STEARIC ACID

STP

SUCCINIC ACID

SUCCINYLATED GLYCERIDES

TARTARIC ACID

TAURINE

TETRAPOTASSIUM PHOSPHATE

TETRASODIUM PYROPHOSPHATE

THIAMINE

THIAMINE HYDROCHLORIDE

THIAMINE MONONITRATE

THIAMINE NITRATE

TOCOPHEROLS

TRICALCIUM PHOSPHATE

TRIETHYL CITRATE

TRIGLYCERIDES

TRISODIUM PHOSPHATE

TUMERIC

VANILLIN

VITAMIN A

VITAMIN A ACETATE

VITAMIN A PALMITATE

VITAMIN B_1

VITAMIN B_2

VITAMIN B_6

VITAMIN B_{12}

VITAMIN C

VITAMIN D_2

VITAMIN D_3

VITAMIN E

VITAMIN K$_1$

VITAMIN K$_2$

WHEY SOLIDS

XANTHAN GUM

ACESULFAME POTASSIUM

ACESULFAME-K

ACETIC ACID

ALGAE

ALGIN

ALGIN DERIVATIVE

ALGIN GUM

ALGINIC ACID

AMMONIUM ALGINATE

AMMONIUM SULFATE

ARTIFICIAL FLAVORING

ASPARTAME

BENZOATE OF SODA

BENZOIC ACID

BENZOYL PEROXIDE

CALCIUM ALGINATE

CALCIUM CARRAGEENAN

CALCIUM DISODIUM EDTA

CARNAUBA WAX

CAROB BEAN GUM

CAROB SEED GUM

CARRAGEENAN

COPPER CARBONATE

COPPER GLUCONATE

COPPER SULFATE

CORN SWEETENER

CORN SYRUP

COTTONSEED OIL

DEXTROSE

DIOCTYL SODIUM SULFOSUCCINATE

FERROUS GLUCONATE

FERROUS SULFATE

FRUCTOSE

FRUIT SUGAR

GLUCOSE

GUAR GUM

HIGH FRUCTOSE CORN SYRUP

HYDROGENATED VEGETABLE OIL

INVERT SUGAR

IRON

LOCUST BEAN GUM

MAGNESIUM CHLORIDE

MAGNESIUM OXIDE

MAGNESIUM SILICATE

METHYLPARABEN

MODIFIED FOOD STARCH

NIACIN

NIACINAMIDE

NICOTINIC ACID

NUTRASWEET

OLESTRA

PALM OIL

PHOSPHORIC ACID

POTASSIUM ALGINATE

POTASSIUM SULFATE

PROPYLENE GLYCOL ALGINATE

PROPYLPARABEN

SIMPLESSE

SMOKE FLAVORING

SODIUM ALGINATE

SODIUM BENZOATE

SODIUM BISULFATE

SODIUM CHLORIDE

SODIUM SULFATE

St. John's Bread

SUCROSE

SULFURIC ACID

Sunette

TABLE SALT

TABLE SUGAR

TBHQ

TERTIARY BUTYLHYDROQUINONE

VINEGAR ACID

XYLITOL

ALUMINUM AMMONIUM SULFATE

ALUMINUM CHLORIDE

ALUMINUM HYDROXIDE

ALUMINUM OLEATE

ALUMINUM PALMITATE

ALUMINUM POTASSIUM SULFATE

ALUMINUM SULFATE

AMMONIUM SULFITE

ARTIFICIAL COLOR

BHA

BHT

BROMINATED VEGETABLE OIL

BUTYLATED HYDROXYANISOLE

BUTYLATED HYDROXYTOLUENE

BVO

CAFFEINE

CALCIUM SACCHARIN

MENADIONE

MONOSODIUM GLUTAMATE

MSG

POTASSIUM BISULFITE

POTASSIUM BROMATE

POTASSIUM METABISULFITE

POTASSIUM NITRATE

POTASSIUM PYROSULFITE

POTASSIUM SULFITE

PROPYL GALLATE

QUININE

QUININE HYDROCHLORIDE

QUININE SULFATE

SACCHARIN

SODIUM BISULFITE

SODIUM METABISULFITE

SODIUM NITRATE

SODIUM NITRITE

SODIUM SACCHARIN

SODIUM SULFITE

SULPHUR DIOXIDE

VITAMIN K_3

Glossary

ACIDIFIER

Changes the degree of acidity. Also used to add tartness. Can also act as a flavor enhancer.

ACIDULANT

An acid added to food to aid in processing. Fights bacteria, lowers pH levels, thus aiding in the sterilization of canned food. Acts as a sequestrant.

ADJUVANT

A secondary ingredient used to intensify the main ingredient in food.

ALKALI

Helps retain flavor by controlling a food's pH level. It also removes excess acidity.

ANTIBROWNING AGENT

Inhibits the discoloration of fruit exposed to oxygen.

ANTICAKING AGENT

Helps powdered substances avoid getting lumpy from moisture.

ANTIOXIDANT

Controls the breakdown or oxidizing of fatty acids, thus preventing food from becoming rancid.

ANHYDROUS

A term used to describe the characteristic of containing no water.

ARTIFICIAL

A term used to describe a substance that is chemically synthesized and cannot be duplicated by nature.

BLEACHING AGENT

Used primarily in flour to expedite a natural aging process that occurs during storage. Aging causes flour to become white and helps dough rise faster. Because natural aging is cost prohibitive, bleaching and other aging agents are used.

BUFFER

Neutralizes acidity or alkalinity.

CARCINOGEN

Cancer causing substance.

CLARIFYING AGENT

Filters or clarifies alcoholic beverages and vinegar.

CURING AGENT
Used to stabilize color, give flavor, or preserve.

DEFOAMING AGENT
Reduces foaming during cooking and processing.

DERIVATIVE
A substance made from another substance.

DISPERSING AGENT
Used to promote uniform separation.

DOUGH CONDITIONER
Improves the consistency of dough for easier handling during processing. Adds to the palatability of bread and baked goods.

EMULSIFIER
Used to help keep ingredients such as vinegar and oil in salad dressing from separating.

ENZYME

Affects a biological change in food.

FERMENTATION

A chemical change to break down energy-rich compounds by the action of bacteria, yeast, etc.

FIRMING AGENT

Added to canned vegetables, for example, to keep them crisp.

FIXATIVE

Added to meat to maintain reddish appearance.

FLAVOR ENHANCER

Usually a salt-based compound with little or no taste of its own which intensifies flavor.

FORTIFIED

The addition of nutrients such as vitamins and minerals to products such as cereal and imitation fruit drinks.

GLAZE OR GLAZING AGENT

A resin used to coat candies to give them a shiny appearance.

HUMECTANT

Added to food to maintain moisture by actually attracting water from the air.

LEAVENING AGENT

Used in dough to make it rise by chemical reaction.

METABOLISM

The process by which food is transformed to energy in the body.

MUTAGEN

A substance that can cause change, especially genetic change.

NEUTRALIZER

Neutralizes or adjusts the acidity of food.

NUTRITIONAL SUPPLEMENT

Nutrients used as replacements or additions to those available in food.

OLEORESIN

An oil or resin that contains the essential characteristic of its source. Adds flavor or color to food.

PLASTICIZER

Makes food flexible, thus more manageable during processing.

PRESERVATIVE

Hinders unwanted biological changes in food.

PROPELLANT

Gas used to force contents from an aerosol container.

SEQUESTRANT

Neutralizes the unwanted effects of metals, such as rancidity in fats and oils.

SOLUBLE

Capable of completely dissolving in fluid.

STABILIZER

Promotes uniformity by preventing separation.

SYNTHETIC

Artificially made; not natural.

TEXTURIZER

Used to give a desirable consistency or texture to food.

TOXIC

Poisonous.

Bibliography

BOOKS

Block, Zenas
It's All On the Label
Boston/Toronto: Little, Brown and Company 1981

Buist, Robert, Ph.D.
Food Chemical Sensitivity
New York: Avery 1988

Freydberg, Nicholas, Ph.D.
and Willis A. Gortner, Ph.D.
The Food Additives Book
New York: Bantam 1982

Boldface indicates recommended reading

Green, Nancy Sokol
Poisoning Our Children;
Surviving in a Toxic World
Chicago: The Noble Press 1991

Hawley's Condensed Chemical Dictionary
New York: Van Nostrand Reinhold 1987

Hunter, Beatrice Trum
Additives Book
Connecticut: Keats Publishing 1980

Jacobson, Michael F.
Eater's Digest; The Consumer's
Factbook of Food Additives
New York: Doubleday and Company 1976

Jones, Julie Miller
Food Safety
Eagan Press 1992

Machlin, L.J.
Handbook of Vitamins: Nutritional,
Biochemical, and Clinical Aspects.
New York: Marcel Dekker, Inc. 1991

Mindell, Earl
Unsafe at Any Meal
New York: Warner Books 1987

Smolinski, Susan C.
Handbook of Food, Drug & Cosmetic Excipients
CRC Press 1992

Winter, Ruth
**A Consumer's Dictionary of
Food Additives**
New York: Crown Publishers 1989

Boldface indicates recommended reading

GOVERNMENT SOURCES

The Office of the Federal Register,
National Archives and Records
Administration, Washington, DC 1990
FDA Code of Federal Regulations
Parts 1 through 199

ARTICLES

A Consumer's Guide to Food Labels
FDA Consumer Magazine, (April 1990)
DHHS Publication No. (FDA) 90-2083

Lehmann, Phyllis
**More Than You Ever Thought You'd
Know About Food Additives**
FDA Consumer Magazine, (February, 1982)
DHHS Publication No. (FDA) 82-2160

Lehmann, Phyllis
**More Than You Ever Thought You'd
Know About Food Additives**
FDA Consumer Magazine, (June 1979)
DHHS Publication No. (FDA) 79-2119

Lehmann, Phyllis
**More Than You Ever Thought You'd
Know About Food Additives**
FDA Consumer Magazine, (April 1979)
DHHS Publication No. (FDA) 79-2115

A Primer on Food Additives
FDA Consumer Magazine, (October, 1988)
DHHS Publication No. (FDA) 89-2227

Blumenthal, Dale
A New Look at Food Labeling
FDA Consumer Magazine, (November, 1989)
DHHS Publication No. (FDA) 89-2228

Journal of the American Medical Association
 (June, 1985)
Vol. 253. No. 23

Lecos, Chris W.
Food Labels
FDA Consumer Magazine, (March, 1988)
DHHS Publication

Larkin, Timothy
Food Additives and Hyperactive Children
FDA Consumer Magazine, (March, 1977)
DHHS Publication No. (FDA) 77-2080

Larkin, Timothy
Exploring Food Additives
FDA Consumer Magazine, (June, 1976)
DHHS Publication No. (FDA) 76-2020

CHRONIMED Publishing Books of Related Interest

The Healthy Eater's Guide to Family & Chain Restaurants by Hope S. Warshaw, M.M.Sc., R.D. Here's the only guide that tells you how to eat healthier in over 100 of America's most popular family and chain restaurants. It offers complete and up-to-date nutrition information and suggests which items to choose and avoid.

004214, ISBN 1-56561-017-2 $9.95

The Label Reader's Pocket Dictionary of Food Additives by Mike Lapchick with Cindy Appleseth, R.Ph., is the only quick-reference guide to more than 250 of today's most common food additives– found in virtually everything we eat. It has the latest findings in an easy-to-read dictionary format with all the information you'll need to make intelligent food decisions.

004224, ISBN 1-56561-027-X $4.95

One Year of Healthy, Hearty, and Quick One-Dish Meals by Pam Spaude and Jan Owan-McMenamin, R.D., is a collection of 365 easy-to-make healthy and tasty family favorites and unique creations that are meals in themselves. Most of the dishes take under 30 minutes to prepare.

004217, ISBN 1-56561-019-9 $12.95

Let Them Eat Cake by Virginia N. White with Rosa A. Mo, R.D. If you're looking for delicious and healthy pies, cookies, puddings, and cakes, this book will give you your just desserts. With easy, step-by-step instructions, this innovative cookbook features complete nutrition information, the latest exchange values, and tips on making your favorite snacks more healthful.

004206, ISBN 1-56561-011-3 $12.95

Beyone Alfalfa Sprouts and Cheese: The Healthy Meatless Cookbook by Judy Gilliard and Joy Kirkpatrick, R.D., includes creative and savory meatless dishes using ingredients found in just about every grocery store. It also contains helpful cooking tips, complete nutrition information, and the latest exchange values.

004218, ISBN 1-56561-020-2 $12.95

All-American Low-Fat Meals in Minutes by M.J. Smith, M.A., R.D., L.D. Filled with tantalizing recipes and valuable tips, this cookbook makes great-tasting low-fat foods a snap for holidays, special occasions, or everyday. Most recipes take only minutes to prepare.

004079, ISBN 0-937721-73-5 $12.95

The Guiltless Gourmet by Judy Gilliard and Joy Kirkpatrick, R.D. A perfect fusion of sound nutrition and creative cooking, this book is loaded with delicious recipes high in flavor and low in fat, sugar, calories, cholesterol, and salt.

004021, ISBN 0-937721-23-9 $9.95

The Guiltless Gourmet Goes Ethnic by Judy Gilliard and Joy Kirkpatrick, R.D. More than a cookbook, this sequel to *The Guiltless Gourmet* shows how easy it is to lower the sugar, calories, sodium, and fat in your favorite ethnic dishes—without sacrificing taste.

004072, ISBN 0-937721-68-9 $11.95

European Cuisine from the Guiltless Gourmet by Judy Gilliard and Joy Kirkpatrick, R.D. This book shows you how to lower the sugar, salt, cholesterol, total fat, and calories in delicious Greek, English, German, Russian, and Scandinavian dishes. Plus it features complete nutrition information and the latest exchange values.

004085, ISBN 0-937721-81-6 $11.95

The Joy of Snacks by Nancy Cooper, R.D. Offers more than 200 delicious recipes and nutrition information for hearty snacks, including sandwiches, appetizers, soups, spreads, cookies, muffins, and treats especially for kids. The book also suggests guidelines for selecting convenience snacks and interpreting information on food labels.

004086, ISBN 0-937721-82-4 $12.95

Convenience Food Facts by Arlene Monk, R.D., C.D.E., with Marion Franz, R.D., M.S. C.D.E. Includes complete nutrition information, tips, and exchange values on more than 1,500 popular name-brand processed foods commonly found in grocery store freezers and shelves. Helps you plan easy-to-prepare, nutritious meals.

004081, ISBN 0-937721-77-8 $10.95

Fast Food Facts by Marion Franz, R.D., M.S. This revised and up-to-date best-seller shows how to make smart nutrition choices at fast food restaurants—and tells what to avoid. Includes complete nutrition information on more than 1,000 menu offerings from the 21 largest fast food chains.
Standard-size edition 004068, ISBN 0-937721-67-0 $6.95
Pocket edition   004073, ISBN 0-937721-69-7 $4.95

Exchanges for All Occasions by Marion Franz, R.D., M.S. Exchanges and meal planning suggestions for just about any occasion, sample meal plans, special tips for people with diabetes, and more.

004003, ISBN 0-937721-22-0 $12.95

Fight Fat & Win by Elaine Moquette-Magee, R.D., M.P.H. This breakthrough book explains how to easily incorporate low-fat dietary guidelines into every modern eating experience, from fast-food and common restaurants to quick meals at home, simply by making smarter choices.

004070, ISBN 0-937721-65-4 $9.95

CHRONIMED Publishing
P.O. Box 47945
Minneapolis, MN 55447-9727

Please send me the books I have checked above. I am
enclosing $_____. (Please add $3.00 to this order
to cover postage and handling. Minnesota residents add 6.5%
sales tax.) Send check or money order, no cash or C.O.D.'s.
Prices are subject to change without notice.

Name ⎯⎯⎯⎯⎯⎯⎯⎯⎯⎯⎯⎯⎯⎯⎯⎯⎯⎯⎯⎯⎯

Address ⎯⎯⎯⎯⎯⎯⎯⎯⎯⎯⎯⎯⎯⎯⎯⎯⎯⎯⎯⎯

City ⎯⎯⎯⎯⎯⎯⎯⎯⎯ State ⎯⎯ Zip ⎯⎯⎯⎯

Allow 4 to 6 weeks for delivery.
Quantity discounts available upon request.
Or order by phone: 1-800-848-2793,
1-800-444-5951 (non-metro area of Minnesota)
612-546-1146 (Minneapolis/St. Paul metro area).
Please have your credit card number ready.